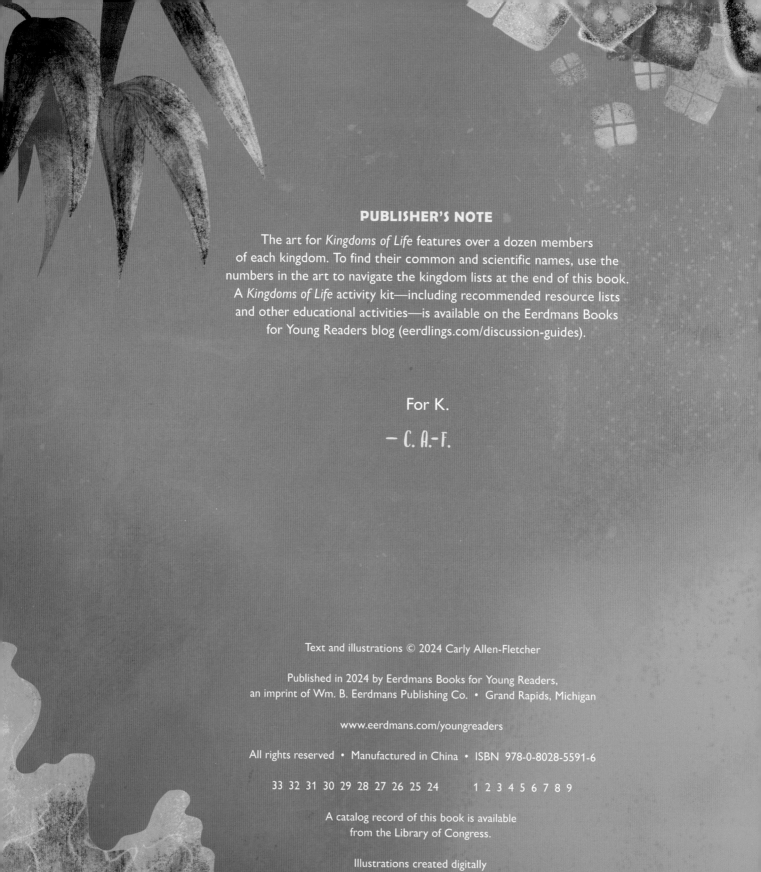

PUBLISHER'S NOTE

The art for *Kingdoms of Life* features over a dozen members of each kingdom. To find their common and scientific names, use the numbers in the art to navigate the kingdom lists at the end of this book. A *Kingdoms of Life* activity kit—including recommended resource lists and other educational activities—is available on the Eerdmans Books for Young Readers blog (eerdlings.com/discussion-guides).

For K.

— C. A.-F.

Text and illustrations © 2024 Carly Allen-Fletcher

Published in 2024 by Eerdmans Books for Young Readers,
an imprint of Wm. B. Eerdmans Publishing Co. • Grand Rapids, Michigan

www.eerdmans.com/youngreaders

33 32 31 30 29 28 27 26 25 24   1 2 3 4 5 6 7 8 9

A catalog record of this book is available
from the Library of Congress.

Illustrations created digitally

Eerdmans Books for Young Readers would like to thank
Jill Holz (B.S. Geology and Geophysics, M.Ed., and
National Geographic Certified Educator) for sharing her
scientific expertise on Earth's life-forms.

FSC
www.fsc.org

MIX
Paper | Supporting
responsible forestry
FSC® C104723

KINGDOMS OF LIFE

written and illustrated by

CARLY ALLEN-FLETCHER

EERDMANS BOOKS FOR YOUNG READERS

GRAND RAPIDS, MICHIGAN

Life is all around us.

In the sky, the sea, and the soil, life exists in millions of different, incredible ways.

Life is anything that grows, reproduces, and feeds.

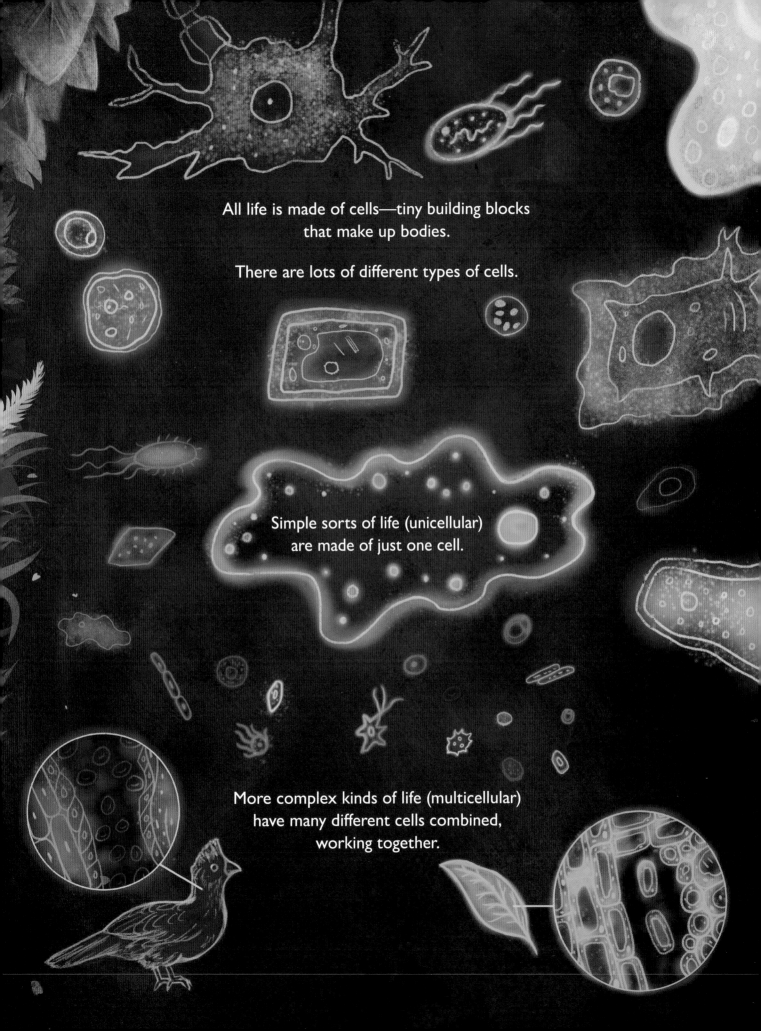

All life is made of cells—tiny building blocks
that make up bodies.

There are lots of different types of cells.

Simple sorts of life (unicellular)
are made of just one cell.

More complex kinds of life (multicellular)
have many different cells combined,
working together.

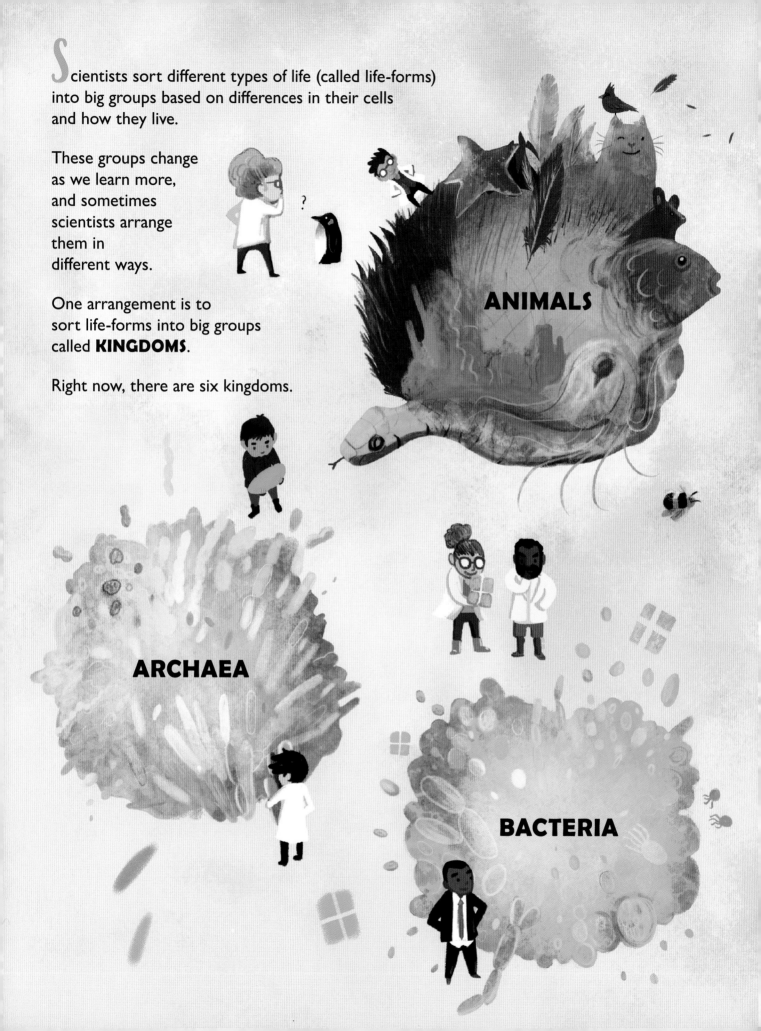

Scientists sort different types of life (called life-forms) into big groups based on differences in their cells and how they live.

These groups change as we learn more, and sometimes scientists arrange them in different ways.

One arrangement is to sort life-forms into big groups called **KINGDOMS**.

Right now, there are six kingdoms.

ANIMALS

ARCHAEA

BACTERIA

PLANTS

FUNGI

PROTISTS

Let's take a closer look
at each one of these kingdoms.

ANIMALS

This is the most complex group of life-forms. The animal kingdom is full of all kinds of creatures in all shapes and sizes: tiny sea creatures, huge elephants, wriggling worms, soaring birds—and you! Despite all this variety, animals do have some things in common.

Animals get energy by eating other life-forms and reproduce by sharing cells to create new life. Some lay eggs or give birth to babies—and some can split themselves into copies and reproduce that way.

They all have some way of moving—whether by legs, wings, fins, or wiggling along. All animals are born, grow older, and eventually die.

Animals live all over the world and have found ways to adapt to all types of conditions. Camels survive in the harsh desert by storing nutritious fat in their humps and water in their bloodstream. Antarctic fish have special antifreeze-like blood to keep them from freezing in icy water.

Different types of animals vary enormously in size. The blue whale, at over 100 ft (30 m) long, is thought to be the biggest animal ever. At the other end of the scale, these fairy wasps are barely 0.2 in (1 mm) long—smaller than a grain of rice!

Even among the same species of animal, there can be lots of variety. Dogs can be as short as a Chihuahua (5–8 in, or 13–20 cm tall), or as tall as an Irish Wolfhound (32–35 in, or 81–89 cm tall).

The members of the animal kingdom have much in common, but they can also surprise us! Here are a few animals with some very special ways of living.

Unlike other animals, this sea slug can make energy from the sun, like plants do. When it is young, it eats a lot of algae, which it absorbs, turning itself green. After that, it can use the algae in its skin to make energy from the sun, and doesn't eat again for the rest of its life!

35

40

In tropical oceans you can see the beautiful and strange "immortal jellyfish." The immortal jellyfish does age—but unlike other life-forms, when it gets old, this fascinating creature can go back to being a baby again.

Scientists think that—as long as the immortal jellyfish doesn't become sick or get eaten—this animal might be able to live forever.

Tardigrades are unusual animals. These tiny creatures (also known as water bears or moss piglets) are extremely tough, even though they're barely bigger than the period at the end of this sentence.

Although they usually like to live on moss, tardigrades have also been found on icy mountains, deep under the sea, and in hot springs. Not only can they survive in these conditions, they can hibernate for decades without food or water. Tardigrades have even survived in space.

These beautiful corals and sea sponges might look more like plants, but they are actually animals. Although neither move around like other animals do, corals have swaying, tentacle-like arms to catch food.

Corals are made of many tiny animals called polyps, joined together in huge groups known as reefs.

Sea sponges and corals might be the world's longest-lived animals. Some have been found that are thousands of years old.

PLANTS

From the green grass beneath your feet,
to floating water lilies and towering redwood
trees, plants come in many different
shapes and sizes.

Through a process called photosynthesis, plants get their energy from sunlight, water, and soil.

Most plants reproduce by spreading seeds.

Although they don't roam around like animals do, plants can move slowly, twisting and growing toward the light. Plants also age differently than animals. While some plants only live a short time, many age very slowly and can live for thousands of years.

Plants grow all over the world, in every type of climate. Cacti store water in their bodies to survive in the desert. Arctic poppies are covered in fine hair that keeps them warm in cold wind.

The tallest individual plant is Hyperion, a redwood tree over 380 ft (116 m) tall.

The smallest is watermeal, a tiny floating plant as small as cupcake sprinkles.

Some plants live in unusual ways.
Most plants create new, different plants
through their seeds, but these
aspen trees reproduce differently.

They are only the surface part of
one giant life-form, with hidden roots
connected underground. This giant aspen
is called Pando, or "the trembling giant."

26

Every tree in this massive grove is
an identical clone, making Pando
the largest—and possibly
oldest—plant in the world.

Unlike most plants, these air plants
don't use their roots to get nutrients from
the soil. They use their leaves to absorb
water and nutrients from the air, and cling
onto rocks or other plants
with their roots.

27

32

The plants to the left are carnivorous,
which means they feed on animals.
Venus flytraps lure in flies, then
close with a snap! The fly
is then slowly digested.

31

30

Waterwheel plants float in lakes
and ponds, trapping tiny creatures for
food. Unlike most plants, which move very
slowly, these plants react very quickly,
snapping their traps shut when triggered.

28

Plants need water to live, but some have found ways to cope with dry conditions. The baobab trees of Africa can hold thousands of gallons of water in their enormous trunks.

29

These resurrection plants have a different survival method. When water runs out, they dry up and curl into a tight ball, then hibernate—not growing or needing food. They can wait for years like this. When the rain returns, they "resurrect" themselves, turning green and growing again.

FUNGI

Mold, mushrooms, and mildew are all types of fungi. Unlike plants, fungi don't move or make their own food. They live by absorbing nutrients from other life-forms such as trees or dead leaves. This helps break down old life, putting nutrients back into ecosystems.

Fungi can reproduce by spreading spores (tiny, simple seeds), splitting into different parts, or combining with each other to create new life. This puffball mushroom spews out millions of spores in a big cloud.

Many fungi have mycelia: long, thin threads that grow underground like tree roots. The part of a fungus we see is only the fruit, like apples on an apple tree. Scientists call this part the "fruiting body."

Fungi like to live in damp places, like forests, caves, and tree roots. There are even tiny fungi that live on corals in the ocean and inside other life-forms.

Many fungi are short-lived, but some grow into huge groups that live for many years. Deep in the forests of Oregon, you can see many clusters of these brown honey mushrooms. They only appear in autumn, and although they seem small on the surface, they are actually part of one of the Earth's biggest life-forms.

Hidden underground, the mycelium of this "humongous fungus" spreads over thousands of acres and has been growing slowly from tree to tree for thousands of years.

20

The hidden mycelia of fungi can be enormous, while the fruiting bodies we see are small—but not always. A bracket fungus was found in China that was over 35 ft (11 m) long, and these edible mushrooms from Africa (called chi-ngulu-ngulu) can be up to 3 ft (1 m) across.

21

22

Most fungi feed on organic matter (material like wood or plants that were once alive), but some have a special diet. Scientists have discovered fungi that can eat plastic, like these oyster mushrooms.

Unlike other types of fungi, these tiny chytrids can move. They live in water all over the world and wriggle along with a type of tail.

23

While many fungi
are harmless, some can be very
dangerous. Mushrooms like this
death cap are poisonous and
deadly if eaten. The mold that grows
on old food is a type of fungi,
and it can make us ill.

Not all mold is bad, though.
Certain types of mold
are used to make cheese,
or even medicine such as
penicillin.

Fungi, especially mushrooms,
are very common in cooking,
but one of the most-used ones
may not be what you think.
Yeast, used for baking breads and
brewing drinks, is a type of tiny fungi.

PROTISTS

Protists are mostly small, simple types of life such as slime and algae—although some are more complex, like kelp. Many protists are microscopic—so small that we can't see them by just using our eyes. We need to use a special tool called a microscope to look closer. Life-forms like this are called microorganisms.

The life-forms in this kingdom are something in between plants, animals, and fungi, with many different characteristics.

Some protists eat other life-forms to survive, like animals do. Others use photosynthesis, like plants, to make their food. Some protists do both.

15

Some protists reproduce by dividing themselves into copies, or by sharing cells with each other to make new life, like animals do. Others send out spores that turn into new life, in the same way that fungi do.

Unlike most plants and fungi, protists can move around. Many have tiny hair-like cilia that they flap to push themselves along. Some do the same but with a flagellum, a longer tail-like structure.

16

18

Some protists can live for many years; others only days. There are protists that split into copies of themselves, over and over again, not aging in the same way as animals or plants.

17

Protists are often found in wet places like swamps, ponds, lakes, and seas. Many types of protists live in the oceans, where they are an important part of the ecosystem, providing food and homes for sea life. Seaweeds (like this sea lettuce) are a common type of protist found in seas and oceans worldwide. Although they look like plants, seaweeds are actually algae.

While many protists are tiny microorganisms, some protists are much bigger.

This giant kelp is a type of seaweed. It is thought to be the biggest protist in the world, growing up to 100 ft (30 m) long. Giant kelp grows in huge underwater forests in cool ocean waters.

19

20

These sailor's eyeballs (algae) are found on tropical reefs. Every colorful bubble is one giant cell.

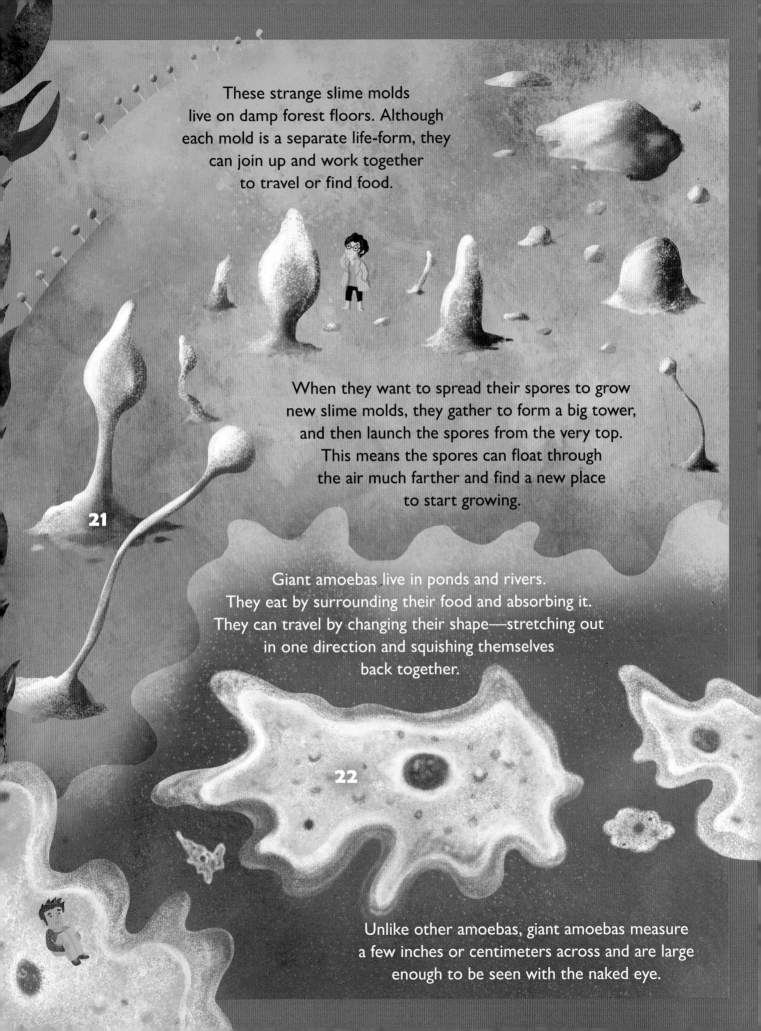

These strange slime molds
live on damp forest floors. Although
each mold is a separate life-form, they
can join up and work together
to travel or find food.

When they want to spread their spores to grow
new slime molds, they gather to form a big tower,
and then launch the spores from the very top.
This means the spores can float through
the air much farther and find a new place
to start growing.

21

Giant amoebas live in ponds and rivers.
They eat by surrounding their food and absorbing it.
They can travel by changing their shape—stretching out
in one direction and squishing themselves
back together.

22

Unlike other amoebas, giant amoebas measure
a few inches or centimeters across and are large
enough to be seen with the naked eye.

BACTERIA

Billions and billions of bacteria surround us every day. They are simple life-forms with only one cell, and are thought to be the most abundant life-forms on Earth. They feed on sunlight, chemicals, and other types of life such as dead plants or animals. Like plants, bacteria make the oxygen we breathe, and keep water and soil full of nutrients so that new life can grow. Scientists are still finding out all the amazing things that bacteria can do.

Like some fungi and protists, bacteria reproduce by splitting themselves in two, over and over again, reproducing millions of times in one day. Like protists, bacteria can move, gliding or swimming along with flagella.

Bacteria come in three main types, organized by shape: rods (bacilli), spirals (spirilla), and spheres (cocci). They arrange themselves in different ways, sometimes making pairs or long chains, or grouping together.

Bacteria don't just live all around us; they live inside us too. Every creature on Earth has bacteria living inside it. Some bacteria can cause illness, but most are beneficial, living in digestive systems and helping to break down food.

As well as helping digest food, bacteria can also make food. It is bacteria that turns milk into yogurt or cheese, and changes vegetables into pickles, kimchi, or sauerkraut. These products are called fermented foods.

Most bacteria are microscopic, but not all.

25

This bacterium, *Epulopiscium fishelsoni*, lives inside tropical surgeonfish, helping them digest food. It is as big as a grain of salt.

26

Thiomargarita namibiensis, also known as the "Sulfur Pearl of Namibia," is found on the seafloor off the coast of Namibia. It is not much bigger than this line: - But that's a giant in the bacteria kingdom! It is named after the shimmering bits of sulfur inside its body.

27

The biggest bacterium of all is *Thiomargarita magnifica*. This long, thin bacteria was discovered very recently in Caribbean mangrove swamps. Each individual cell can grow to over 0.5 in (1.3 cm) in length—thousands of times bigger than most bacteria.

Bacteria often help animals digest food, but they also help this Hawaiian bobtail squid glow.

Aliivibrio fischeri is a bioluminescent bacterium that lives inside this little squid. The bacteria's glow helps the squid blend into the light shining down on the ocean, hiding it from hungry predators. In return, the bacteria get a safe place to live.

28

When two different life-forms live and work together like this, it is called a symbiotic relationship.

ARCHAEA

All around us, so small that they are all invisible
to the naked eye, live archaea. These tiny life-forms
are found all over the world, feeding on gas,
minerals, metals, and sunlight.

Like bacteria, archaea are simple, single-celled life-forms
that multiply by dividing themselves into copies over
and over again. They also move around
using hair-like body parts
called flagella.

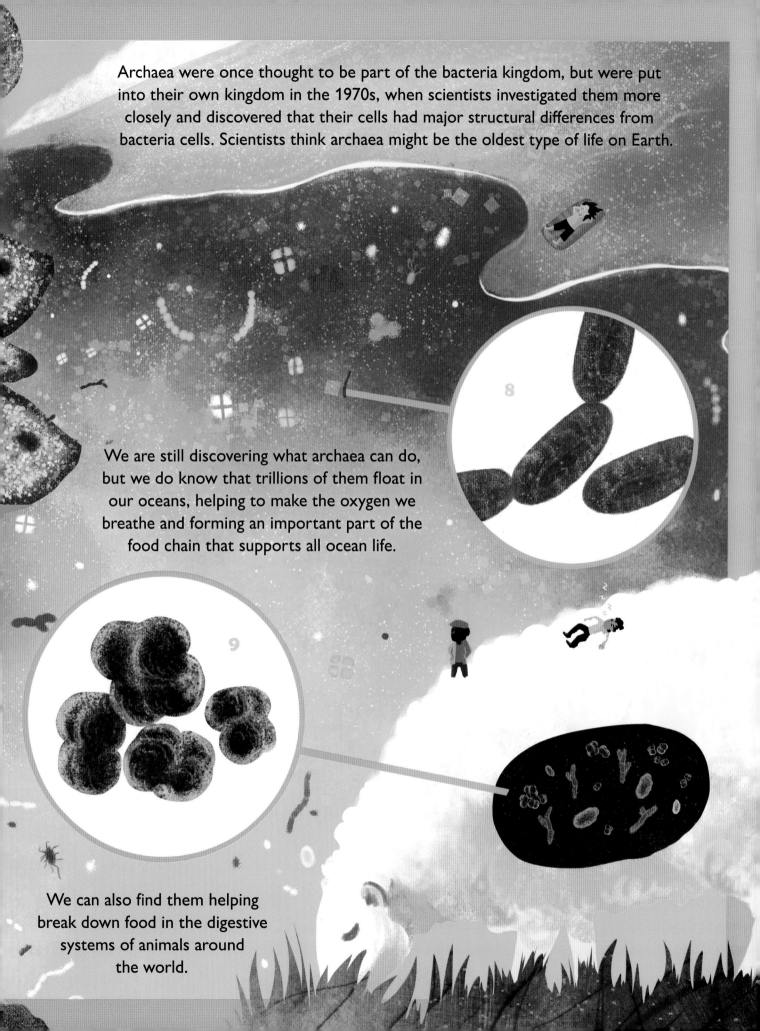

Archaea were once thought to be part of the bacteria kingdom, but were put into their own kingdom in the 1970s, when scientists investigated them more closely and discovered that their cells had major structural differences from bacteria cells. Scientists think archaea might be the oldest type of life on Earth.

We are still discovering what archaea can do, but we do know that trillions of them float in our oceans, helping to make the oxygen we breathe and forming an important part of the food chain that supports all ocean life.

We can also find them helping break down food in the digestive systems of animals around the world.

Although they are tiny, archaea are very tough. They have a strong membrane (like a skin) that protects them from extreme conditions.

Archaea can eat inorganic (non-living) things, such as toxic acid and metals. This means they can survive in places where most other life-forms cannot.

Life-forms that can live in extreme conditions like this are called extremophiles.

10

Deep down on the ocean floor, vents spew super-hot water out into the ocean. Archaea live in these boiling hot waters.

11

12

Far under the ice of the South Pole is a dark, freezing cold lake. Scientists have found archaea here, too.

Some places on Earth—like the famous geysers and hot springs of Yellowstone Park—have water so acidic or alkaline that it is dangerous for most life.

But both bacteria and archaea can live there quite happily. In fact, the beautiful colors of Yellowstone's springs are caused by the archaea and bacteria that live there.

The Dead Sea is too salty for other types of life, but archaea and bacteria can live here too.

Once a life-form has been put into one of the six kingdoms, it is then sorted into smaller and smaller groups whose members share similar characteristics.

Doing this helps us learn more about different life-forms and identify new ones as they are discovered.

CATS
(family Felidae)

subfamily
Pantherinae

TIGER
(*Panthera tigris*)

BIG CATS
(genus *Panthera*)

SMALL CATS
(subfamily Felinae)

LION
(*Panthera leo*)

genus
Octocolobus

genus
Felis

PALLAS'S CAT
(*Otocolobus manul*)

HOUSE CAT
(*Felis catus*)

The study and sorting of life-forms is called taxonomy. It has been practiced by scientists worldwide since ancient times. Some of the oldest research is still used today.

In ancient Egypt, plants and their names were painted on walls and recorded on long scrolls such as the Ebers Papyrus.

The ancient Greek philosopher Aristotle spent many years writing *Historia Animalium* (*History of Animals*).

Scholar al-Dīnawarī, from ninth-century Persia, wrote six volumes called *Kitāb al-nabāt* (*Book of Plants*).

In eighteenth-century China, Jiang Tingxi, Yu Sheng, and Zhang Weibang created *Niaopu* (*Manual of Birds*), a giant book of birds painted on silk.

Carl Linnaeus, a Swedish scholar, wrote *Systema Naturae* (*The System of Nature*) in the eighteenth century. The kingdoms method of classification is based on his work, with many updates.

Scientists carry on the work of those before them: exploring further, discovering more, and updating ideas as they learn new information.

Our world is full of wonders, and there is so much left to discover. We know more about the moon than we do about the deepest parts of our oceans.

Every year, we learn more about our home
and the incredible life-forms we share it with.
What will we discover next?

SCIENTIFIC NAMES

You may have spotted a number by each organism in this book. The lists in this section will help you match those numbers with names of the organisms! We've seen how life-forms are sorted into the six kingdoms—and then into smaller and smaller groups according to the characteristics they share. Scientists use these categories (arranged from general to specific) to organize life-forms:

KINGDOM

▶ **PHYLUM (or DIVISION)**

▶ **CLASS**

▶ **ORDER**

▶ **FAMILY**

▶ **GENUS**

▶ **SPECIES**

Some categories are organized with different terms. For example, *division* is equivalent to *phylum*, but is only used for plants and fungi. Some categories can be broken down into smaller subcategories (like subfamily Pantherinae within family Felidae). The following lists use both common (often-used) names and scientific names for each life-form as relevant.

Since one life-form can have many common names, scientists use special, two-part Latin names (genus name + a specific phrase) to identify individual species. For example:

genus *Homo* [human] + *sapiens* [wise]

= *Homo sapiens*

= humans

This scientific name is called a binomial name and is usually written in *italics*.

Sometimes the life-forms shown in this book represent a broader category, such as a family or an order. No matter what name is listed, these descriptions should give you enough information to research and learn more about the life-forms you've seen and read about in this book!

FEATURED LIFE-FORMS

ANIMALS

1. Brown bear (*Ursus arctos*)
2. Sea urchin (class Echinoidea)
3. Tardigrade (phylum Tardigrada)
4. Trichoplax (*Trichoplax adhaerens*)
5. Moray eel (family Muraenidae)
6. Powdered dancer damselfly (*Argia moesta*)
7. Red wiggler worm (*Eisenia fetida*)
8. Friesian cow (*Bos taurus*)
9. Coelacanth (genus *Latimeria*)
10. Giant pangolin (*Smutsia gigantea*)
11. Humans (*Homo sapiens*)
12. William's dwarf gecko (*Lygodactylus williamsi*)
13. Sea anemone (order Actiniaria)
14. Desert tortoise (*Gopherus agassizii*)
15. Vietnamese mossy frog (*Theloderma corticale*)
16. Orange elephant ear sponge (*Agelas clathrodes*)
17. Common sea fan (*Gorgonia ventalina*)
18. Koala (*Phascolarctos cinereus*)
19. Macaroni penguin (*Eudyptes chrysolophus*)
20. Yellow tube sponge (*Aplysina fistularis*)
21. Quokka (*Setonix brachyurus*)
22. Spanish shawl (*Flabellinopsis iodinea*)
23. Echidna (family Tachyglossidae)
24. Giant clam (genus *Tridacna*)
25. Giant panda (*Ailuropoda melanoleuca*)
26. Corn snake (*Pantherophis guttatus*)
27. Ochre starfish (*Pisaster ochraceus*)
28. Antarctic toothfish (*Dissostichus mawsoni*)
29. Fairy wasp (family Mymaridae)
30. Irish wolfhound (*Canis familiaris*)
31. Chihuahua (*Canis familiaris*)
32. Blue whale (*Balaenoptera musculus*)
33. Bactrian camel (*Camelus bactrianus*)
34. Pajama cardinalfish (*Sphaeramia nematoptera*)
35. Green sea slug (*Elysia chlorotica*)
36. Tardigrade (phylum Tardigrada)
37. Red staghorn coral (*Acropora cervicornis*)
38. Yellow staghorn coral (*Acropora cervicornis*)
39. Yellow tube sponge (*Aplysina fistularis*)
40. Immortal jellyfish (*Turritopsis dohrnii*)

PLANTS

1. Common bamboo (*Bambusa vulgaris*)
2. Aubergine / eggplant (*Solanum melongena*)
3. Apple tree (*Malus domestica*)
4. Common bracken (*Pteridium aquilinum*)
5. White baneberry (*Actaea pachypoda*)
6. Rainbow eucalyptus (*Eucalyptus deglupta*)
7. Carrot (*Daucus carota*)
8. Kentucky bluegrass (*Poa pratensis*)

PLANTS, CONTINUED...

9. Snake plant (*Dracaena trifasciata*)
10. False shamrock (*Oxalis triangularis*)
11. Water lily—leaf (family Nymphaeaceae)
12. Urn haircap (*Pogonatum urnigerum*)
13. Water lily—flower (family Nymphaeaceae)
14. Banana (genus *Musa*)
15. English oak—acorn (*Quercus robur*)
16. Dandelion (genus *Taraxacum*)
17. Saguaro cactus (*Carnegiea gigantea*)
18. Common sunflower (*Helianthus annuus*)
19. Prickly pear cactus (*Opuntia*)
20. Echeveria (genus *Echeveria*)
21. Golden barrel cactus (*Echinocactus grusonii*)
22. Watermeal (genus *Wolffia*)
23. Coast redwood (*Sequoia sempervirens*)
24. Arctic poppy (*Papaver radicatum*)
25. Arctic willow (*Salix arctica*)
26. Eurasian aspen (*Populus tremula*)
27. Air plants (genus *Tillandsia*)
28. Baobab (genus *Adansonia*)
29. Resurrection plant—dried and leafy forms (*Selaginella lepidophylla*)
30. Waterwheel (*Aldrovanda vesiculosa*)
31. Venus flytrap (*Dionaea muscipula*)
32. White-topped pitcher plant (*Sarracenia leucophylla*)

FUNGI

1. Beefsteak fungus (*Fistulina hepatica*)
2. Penicillium (genus *Penicillium*)
3. Baker's yeast (*Saccharomyces cerevisiae*)
4. Bleeding tooth fungus (*Hydnellum peckii*)
5. Aspergillus mold (genus *Aspergillus*)
6. Chicken of the woods (genus *Laetiporus*)
7. Pink parasol mushroom (*Macrolepiota procera*)
8. Cobalt crust fungus (*Terana caerulea*)
9. Spiny woodnight (*Cyptotrama asprata*)
10. Poison fire coral fungus (*Podostroma cornu-damae*)
11. Violet coral fungus (*Clavaria zollingeri*)
12. Shaggy ink cap mushroom (*Coprinus comatus*)
13. Swamp beacon fungus (*Mitrula paludosa*)
14. Pink oyster mushroom (*Pleurotus djamor*)
15. Yellow brain fungus (*Tremella mesenterica*)
16. Mycelium (plural mycelia)—root-like structure of many fungi
17. Cladosporium mold (genus *Cladosporium*)
18. Puffball fungus (genus *Calvatia*)
19. Dark honey mushroom (*Armillaria ostoyae*)
20. Bracket fungus (*Phellinus ellipsoideu*)
21. Chi-ngulu-ngulu (*Termitomyces titanicus*)
22. Oyster mushrooms (*Pleurotus ostraetus*)
23. Chytrids (division Chyrtidiomycota)
24. Penicillium (genus *Penicillium*)
25. Death cap (*Amanita phalloides*)
26. Blue cheese mold (*Penicillium roqueforti*)
27. Baker's yeast (*Saccharomyces cerevisiae*)

PROTISTS

1. Diatom (class Bacillariophyceae)
2. Euglena (*Euglena gracilis*)
3. Wolf's milk slime mold (*Lycogala epidendrum*)
4. Red algae (division Rhodophyta)
5. Scrambled egg slime mold (*Fuligo septica*)
6. *Elaeomyxa cerifera*
7. Actinophryid (order Actinophryid)
8. Giant amoeba (*Chaos carolinensis*)
9. Mermaid's wineglass algae (genus *Acetabularia*)
10. Red raspberry slime mold (*Tubifera ferruginosa*)
11. Orange slime (*Trichia decipiens*)
12. Fresh water algae (genus *Pinnularia*)
13. "The blob" slime mold (*Physarum polycephalum*)
14. Coral slime (*Ceratiomyxa fruticulosa*)
15. *Amoeba proteus*
16. Euglena (*Euglena gracilis*)
17. Sea lettuce (genus *Ulva*)
18. Paramecium (*Paramecium caudatum*)
19. Giant kelp (*Macrocystis pyrifera*)
20. Sailor's eyeballs (*Valonia ventricosa*)
21. Slime mold (*Dictyostelium discoideum*)
22. Giant amoeba (*Chaos carolinensis*)

BACTERIA

1. *Fusobacterium nucleatum*
2. *Vibrio cholerae*
3. *Lactobacillus casei*
4. *Bifidobacterium animalis*
5. *Borrelia burgdorferi*
6. *Streptococcus pyogenes*
7. *Prochlorococcus marinus*
8. *Escherichia coli*
9. *Nocardia asteroides*
10. *Methanobrevibacter smithii*
11. *Lactobacillus delbrueckii*
12. *Deinococcus radiodurans*
13. *Rhizobium leguminosarum*
14. *Corynebacterium diphtheriae*
15. *Actinomyces viscosus*
16. *Micrococcus luteus*
17. *Helicobacter pylori*
18. *Staphylococcus epidermidis*
19. *Weissella koreensis*
20. *Leuconostoc mesenteroides*
21. *Propionibacterium freudenreichi*
22. *Streptococcus thermophilus*
23. *Lactobacillus rhamnosus*
24. *Lactococcus lactis*
25. *Epulopiscium fishelsoni*
26. *Thiomargarita namibiensis*
27. *Thiomargarita magnifica*
28. *Aliivibrio fischeri*

ARCHAEA

1. *Haloquadratum walsbyi*
2. *Planococcus halocryophilus*
3. *Methanococcoides burtonii*
4. Genus *Methanosarcina*
5. *Methanobrevibacter smithii*
6. Genus *Malobacterium*
7. *Staphylothermus marinus*
8. *Halobacterium salinarum*
9. *Methanosarcina barkeri*
10. *Pyrococcus furiosus*
11. *Planococcus halocryophilus*
12. *Methanococcus jannaschii*
13. *Nanopusillus acidilobi*
14. *Sulfolobus acidocaldarius*
15. *Haloquadratum walsbyi*